Leonardo da
VINCI

TELL ME ABOUT

Leonardo da
VINCI

by John Malam

Carolrhoda Books, Inc. / Minneapolis

This edition first published in the United States in 1999 by Carolrhoda Books, Inc.

Copyright © 1998 by Evans Brothers Limited
First published in England in 1998 by Evans Brothers Limited, London

Carolrhoda Books, Inc., c/o The Lerner Publishing Group
241 First Avenue North, Minneapolis, Minnesota 55401 U.S.A.

Website address: www.lernerbooks.com

Library of Congress Cataloging-in-Publication Data

Malam, John.
    Leonardo da Vinci / John Malam.
        p.   cm. — (Tell me about)
    Originally published: London: Evans Brothers, 1998.
    Includes index.
    Summary: A biography of the Italian Renaissance artist and
inventor who was recognized as one of the cleverest men of his time.
    ISBN 1–57505–367–5 (alk. paper)
    1. Leonardo, da Vinci, 1452–1519—Juvenile literature.
2. Artists—Italy—Biography—Juvenile literature. [1. Leonardo,
da Vinci, 1452–1519. 2. Artists.] I. Title. II. Series: Tell me
about (Minneapolis, Minn.)
N6923.L33M355   1999
709'.2—dc21
[B]   98–8489

Printed by Graficas Reunidas SA, Spain
Bound in the United States of America
1 2 3 4 5 6 – OS – 04 03 02 01 00 99

Leonardo da Vinci lived in Italy more than five hundred years ago. He was one of the smartest men of his time. He was an artist and sculptor. He drew designs for machines to fly in the air and sail on the sea, and he discovered many things about how the human body works. This is Leonardo's story.

Leonardo made this drawing of himself when he was about sixty.

Leonardo da Vinci was born on April 15, 1452. He was born in or near the mountain village of Vinci, in central Italy. His name means "Leonardo of Vinci."

The village of Vinci, where Leonardo was born

Leonardo's parents were not married. When Leonardo was very young, he lived with his grandparents.

Leonardo's father married a woman from a rich family. When Leonardo was five, he probably went to live with his father and stepmother.

Vinci is in a part of Italy called Tuscany, where grapes, olives, and vegetables are grown.

From an early age, Leonardo showed great skill as an artist. It is said that the young Leonardo painted a picture of a dragon that was so realistic it scared his father!

When Leonardo was in his teens, his father took him to the city of Florence to meet Andrea del Verrocchio, who was a well-known artist. Verrocchio agreed to teach Leonardo about painting.

The city of Florence was home to many artists. It took all day to get there on horseback from Vinci.

FIORENZA

When Leonardo was about twenty years old, Verrocchio gave him an important job to do. He wanted Leonardo to finish a painting the teacher had started. It was a painting of John the Baptist baptizing Jesus Christ. It needed to have an angel painted on the left side of the picture.

Leonardo painted the angel using oil paints. He probably painted the background, too.

The Baptism of Christ, painted by Verrocchio. The kneeling angel on the left side was painted by Leonardo.

9

Before Leonardo, most artists painted either religious scenes or pictures of important people. Leonardo wanted to be different. He was interested in nature, and so he began to make realistic drawings of the countryside.

Leonardo lived near the river Arno. He made a drawing of it in pen and ink. His picture was full of the feeling of moving water and shadows cast by the trees.

The river Arno

Leonardo's drawing of the valley of the Arno

When Leonardo was thirty, he left Florence and went to work for the duke of Milan. The duke was powerful, and Milan was a great city.

The duke asked Leonardo to make a bronze statue of his father on horseback. Leonardo planned to make the biggest horse statue of all time – over twenty feet tall! But the statue was never completed.

The duke of Milan, Lodovico Sforza, who asked Leonardo to work for him

Leonardo made this sketch of the horse statue.

Before he moved to Milan, Leonardo had written a letter to the duke, asking to work as a designer of weapons. He said he could also build a bridge that could be lifted like a drawbridge.

But the duke wanted Leonardo to work as a painter. The duke wanted to make Milan into a beautiful city, like Florence, and he wanted Leonardo to make his wish come true.

Leonardo wanted to work as an inventor and an artist. He wanted to help the duke in his wars against France and Spain. So the duke made Leonardo his engineer, and Leonardo filled many notebooks with his ideas for inventions.

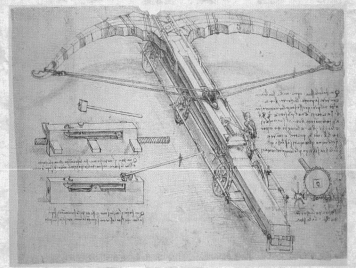

Leonardo sketched this giant crossbow in his notebook. If it had ever been made, it would have been more than eighty feet long.

These are sketches Leonardo made for machines that could be used in war.

Leonardo's ideas for inventions were probably not made into real machines in his lifetime. But after he died, people who read his notebooks found that some of his inventions would work. They made models to prove this.

This gun was built long after Leonardo's death, using designs he drew.

While Leonardo was in Milan, he painted one of the world's great paintings. In a church, on the wall of the monks' dining hall, he painted *The Last Supper*. It shows Jesus Christ and the apostles eating their last meal together.

Leonardo spent about three years on the painting. The monks thought that was too long!

Leonardo's *The Last Supper*. You can see how some paint has flaked off. There are cracks in the wall, too.

After eighteen years in Milan, Leonardo returned to Florence. It was here that he painted his most famous picture.

Leonardo painted a portrait of a young woman. Her name was Mona Lisa. No one is sure who the woman was. Leonardo kept the painting throughout his lifetime. Since then it has been in the Louvre Museum in Paris.

There are many reasons the *Mona Lisa* is a great painting. The woman's eyes have a thoughtful, faraway look, and her mouth has a faint, mysterious smile.

Leonardo's genius as an inventor can be seen in his ideas for flying machines. He studied birds and bats, then made drawings of their wings and how they worked. This gave him the idea for a machine that looked like a giant wing, powered by a man pedaling underneath it.

Leonardo's sketch of his human-powered flying machine

This model shows how Leonardo's flying machine was supposed to look. Its wings would have been covered with cloth. In reality, the machine would have been too heavy to fly.

In his later years, Leonardo was persuaded to return to Milan, where he was asked to paint pictures for King Louis XII of France.

Another artist painted this picture of King Louis XII of France.

Leonardo's *The Virgin and Child with St. Anne* was painted in about 1510.

As Leonardo grew older, he became more and more interested in the human body. He cut up many dead bodies and made detailed drawings of their working parts. He wanted to find out how the heart, brain, eyes, arms, legs, and muscles worked. He wanted to study the body through all its stages, from birth until death.

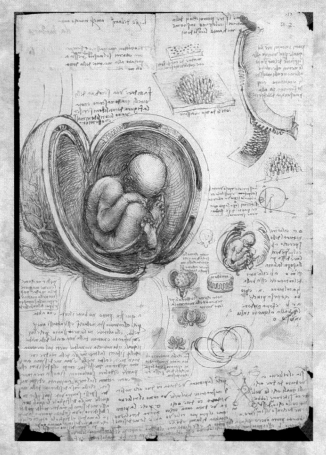

Leonardo's drawing of a baby in its mother's womb

(Right) Leonardo began some paintings by making full-size drawings of them in charcoal. This may have been a sketch for *The Virgin and Child with St. Anne.*

When Leonardo was in his sixties, the new king of France asked him to come and live in France and make paintings for the royal household.

Leonardo lived in France for the last years of his life. There he continued to write notes, make drawings, and conduct experiments. When he died in 1519, at sixty-seven, he left behind thousands of pages of notes and drawings, and some of the most beautiful paintings the world has ever seen.

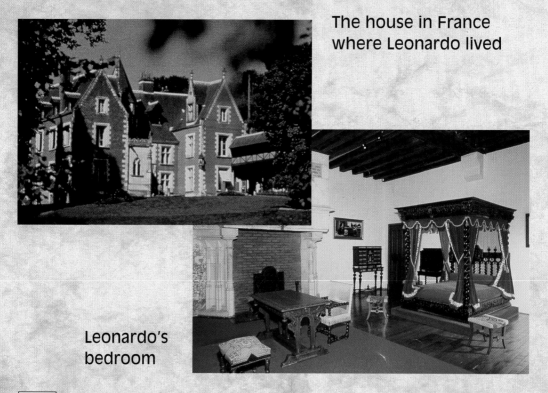

The house in France where Leonardo lived

Leonardo's bedroom

Important Dates

The letter *c* before a date means "about."

1452   Leonardo was born in Vinci, in central Italy

c. 1467   Joined the workshop of Andrea del Verrocchio, in Florence

1482   Moved to Milan to work for Duke Ludovico Sforza

1485   Made his first designs for flying machines

1490   Worked on a giant bronze statue of a horse

1497   Finished painting *The Last Supper*

1499   Left Milan

1500   Returned to Florence

1504   Father died

c. 1505   Started painting the *Mona Lisa*

c. 1506   Returned to Milan

c. 1510   Finished painting *The Virgin and Child with St. Anne*

1516   Moved to France

1519   Leonardo died in France

Leonardo, who was left-handed, wrote backwards, perhaps so he wouldn't smudge the ink.

Key Words

artist
someone who makes drawings and pictures

charcoal
partly burned wood used for drawing

portrait
a picture of a person

sculptor
someone who carves figures out of stone

sketch
a rough drawing, made quickly

Index

Acknowledgments

The author and publisher gratefully acknowledge the following for permission to reproduce copyrighted material:
Cover and back cover AKG
Title page AKG
page 5 AKG **page 6** Robert Harding Picture Library **page 7** Robert Harding Picture Library **page 8** Museo de Firenze com'era/Bridgeman Art Library **page 9** Galleria Degli Uffizi, Florence/Bridgeman Art Library **page 10** (bottom left) AKG (top right) Gavin Hellier/Robert Harding Picture Library **page 11** (bottom left) The Royal Collection © Her Majesty Queen Elizabeth II (top right) Mary Evans Picture Library **page 12** Biblioteca Ambrosiana/Bridgeman Art Library **page 13** (top) e.t. archive (bottom) 'Photos loaned by kind permission of Clos Lucé, home of Leonardo da Vinci' **page 14** AKG **page 15** AKG **page 16** (left) e.t. archive (right) Topham Picturepoint **page 17** (left) Louvre, Paris/Bridgeman Art Library (right) Bibliotheque Nationale, Paris/Bridgeman Art Library **page 18** The Royal Collection © Her Majesty Queen Elizabeth II **page 19** National Gallery, London/Bridgeman Art Library **page 20** Photos loaned by kind permission of Clos Lucé, home of Leonardo da Vinci' **page 21** Science Museum/Science and Society Picture Library

About the Author

John Malam has a degree in ancient history and archeology from the University of Birmingham in England. He is the author of many children's books on topics that include history, natural history, natural science, and biography. Before becoming a writer and editor, he directed archeological excavations. Malam lives in Manchester, England, with his wife, Hilary, and their children, Joseph and Eve.